Nancy Coo Walks 500 sMiles

Meet gentle and ginger Nancy Coo; NC for short,
Alone in her field, sadness she must thwart,
For she has lost the capital 'S' from her S-mile,
To find her capital 'S' she'll search 500 miles.

At Rogie Falls the leaping Salmon she asks,
Toward Strath Bran and the Red Deer they
task.

"You've lost your capital 'S' " the red deer sympathise,
They counsel, "To Belach-Na-Ba" with a twinkle in their eyes.

NC walks up the high Pass of the Cattle,
Warm, with her two coats of fur, it's a bit of a battle,
At the summit a pair of Golden Eagle advise,
"Follow the footsteps of the Saint. Find what you prize".

Enticed to the glittering deep waters of Loch Maree,
She paddles out to the sacred isle and its fallen money tree,
No capital 'S' does she find on this holy island,
Undaunted NC returns to the quest around the Highlands.

The silent Fairy Lochs of Shieldaig now do beckon,
A prayer she whispers, as she walks through the bracken.

Orca and Minke in the Gair-loch delicately enquire,
"NC what is it you seek? What's your heart's desire?"

NC is now accompanied by Melvaig's shy Ghillie Dhu,
The red squirrels assist them both, at the Gardens of Inverewe.

Northwards they point, Ullapool, Summer Isles and beyond,
"Your capital 'S' over Kylesku Bridge did abscond!".

The kind Ghillie Dhu bids Nancy Coo farewell with a cuddle,
That night, snuggling with woolly sheep, she does huddle.

The Old Man of Stoer advises her wisely and sagely,
"Actually last seen was your capital 'S' at 'S'moo cave, now go safely!"

NC arrived to find her capital 'S' had moved onward,
Passing Dounreay, cheerful Otter encourage her forward,
At John-O-Groats the signposts for Nancy Coo are misleading,
Thankfully Puffins from Dunnet Head, help in their reading.

Sprightly, NC hoofed it down the steep steps of Whaligoe,
Her capital 'S' wasn't hiding there. Her ascent? Naturally slow.

At the Hill-O-Many-Stanes tired Nancy Coo
slept deeply,
Northern Lights dancing, fairies protecting her
discreetly.

Dunrobin Castle she searched high and low,
Kindly assisted by Raven and Hooded Crow.

Wolf Stone and Shandwick Stone no capital 'S'
did shelter,
The warm summer sun shone; Nancy Coo started
to swelter.

TO MARK THE PLACE NEAR WHICH
THE LAST WOLF IN SUTHERLAND
WAS KILLED
BY THE HUNTER POLSON
IN OR ABOUT THE YEAR 1700
THIS STONE WAS ERECTED BY
HIS GRACE THE DUKE OF PORTLAND KG
AD 1924

Refreshments she enjoyed at distillery and brewery,
She danced as she walked with much singing and tomfoolery.

The Peregrines perched on the oil-rigs floating at Nigg Bay,
And far travelled Red Kites encourage NC "don't delay".

The Bottlenose Dolphins at Chanonry Point frolicking in the Firth,
Encouraging Nancy Coo, "Visit the Fairy Glen, for magical fairy mirth."

She stayed overnight, the enchanted forest's ginger guest,
Many adventures and new friends. Nancy Coo is surely blessed!

The magic continued as she explored the standing stones at Clava Cairns,
Ancient battle cries of Culloden, Tartan Highlanders, English in coats-of-arms.

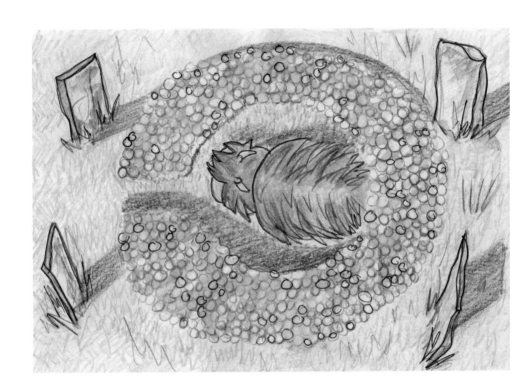

Inverness Castle, St Andrew's Cathedral, more warm Highland "Hellos!"
Then in the distance, Nancy Coo heard Heilan Coo's welcoming bellows.

Nessie greeted, "Failte!" while delighting tourists at Urquhart Castle,
NC trotted quickly past, tourists' photos, at this moment a hassle!

Her Heilan Coo fold in the distant green clover field she saw,
Brothers, Sisters, Cousins, Aunty, Uncle, her Faither and Maw.

Bellowing with joy, forward Nancy Coo ran,
For ahead was her family, friends, her Clan!
For 500 miles Nancy Coo had sought her missing
capital 'S' from her Smile,
Now she recognised, her Smile had been inside
her all the while!

NC's 500 sMile walk around the Highlands of Scotland

1. Inverness - the capital city of the Highlands.
2. Rogie Falls - where leaping salmon can be seen.
3. Strath Bran - the valley of Achnasheen. Achnasheen was an old 'stance' when Heilan Coos were being 'drove' to the cattle markets, 'Trysts' of Dingwall, Muir of Ord, Crieff and Falkirk.
4. Bealach-Na-Ba - the High Pass of the Cattle, ancient drover's pass.
5. Loch Maree - the footsteps of the Saint belong to Saint Máelrubai. This Saint founded the monastery of Applecross. Isle Maree has the remains of a chapel, graveyard, holy well, and holy tree on it.
6. Fairy Lochs of Shieldaig - crash site of an American WWII bomber.
7. Gair-loch- Minke Whales, Orca, Basking Shark, dolphin, seal and porpoise love the waters around Gairloch.
8. Melvaig - The Ghillie Dhu is the kind black fairy of Melvaig who saves and cares for the lost.
9. Inverewe Gardens - gorgeous gardens where red squirrels have been reintroduced.
10. Ullapool - a lovely harbour town where you can catch a ferry to Lewis.
11. Summer Isles - beautiful islands at the mouth of Loch Broom.
12. Kylesku Bridge - a distinctively curved and beautiful bridge.
13. Old Man of Stoer - 60 metre high sea stack with the 'face of a man'. Near Stoer Lighthouse.
14. Smoo Cave - an amazing sea cave in Durness.
15. Dounreay - nuclear facilities.
16. John-O-Groats - nearly the most northerly point of mainland Great Britain.

17. Dunnet Head - the most northerly point of the mainland of Great Britain. Dunnet Head RSPB nature reserve is home to puffins and many more amazing seabirds.
18. Whaligoe Steps - 365 steps that descend to what is a naturally formed harbour.
19. Hill-O-Many Stanes - 200 magical standing stones.
20. Wolf Stone - 2 miles north of Brora.
21. Shandwick Stone - Pictish Stone discovered in 1776.
22. Dunrobin Castle - Stately home and seat of Clan Sutherland.
23. Nigg Bay - A beautiful bay on Cromarty Firth, where Oil Riggs are fabricated. Peregrine falcons now nest on the Riggs.
24. Distillery and Brewery - Easter Ross is world famous for its breweries and distilleries.
25. Chanonry Point - one of the best spots in Scotland to spot Bottlenose Dolphins from land.
26. Fairy Glen - A beautiful Glen with magical broadleaf woods.
27. Clava Cairns - Bronze Age chambers and standing stones, East of Inverness.
28. Culloden - an ancient battlefield and fantastic visitor experience.
29. Inverness Castle and St Andrew's Cathedral - located in Inverness town centre.
30. Urquhart Castle - Medieval Castle located on the shores of Loch Ness.
31. Nessie - The friendly and elusive Loch Ness Monster.
33. Heilan Coo Fold - Highland Cow Herd, however a group of Heilan Coo are never a Herd but a Fold.

About Mandy

Mandy lives in 'The Last House before the Lighthouse' in the remote West Highlands of Scotland.

She lives with her ginger chickens, The Weasleys, Araucana Amy and five ducks, Her Royal Duckesses named Argyll, Sutherland, Ross, Cromarty and Fife.

Mandy loves to write and illustrate books about the wonders of the Highlands where she is surrounded by Haggis friendly habitat.

Mandy protects several secret local Haggii holts.

Books by Mandy

Scottish Beastie Books
Haggis History & Facts
Midge Myths & Facts
Puffin Parable & Facts

Gracie MacKay and her Toothfairie

Buy Further Books at:
Web: www.mandyerush.me
Email: mandyerush@me.com

nancy coo's 500 mile journey

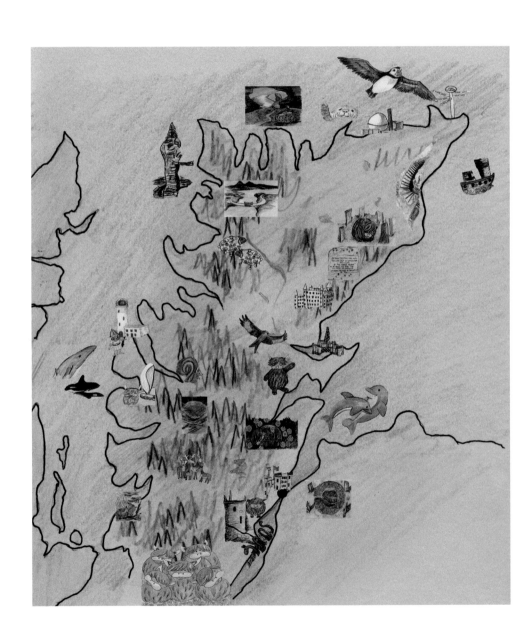